Wednesdays in Marblehead

An exploration of the beauty of Marblehead, Massachusetts

A selection of images from **wednesdaysinmhd.com**

Eyal Oren

DEDICATION

To my incredible wife Heather, who never hesitated with a "Yes, dear"

when I asked to run out for a sunrise or sunset shoot, and who suffered the recurring question,

"Which image do you think is better?" I could not imagine a life without you

and I am so thankful for your love and support.

To my children, who put up with my unending quest to photograph nearly every

moment of your lives. You have brought such incredible joy to our family,

and I am in awe of the amazing individuals you are becoming with each passing year.

ACKNOWLEDGMENT

This book would never have seen the light of day without a great many people.
Thank you to my book designer, Amy Drinker, and copy editor, Becky Burckmyer,
without whom this book would not have been as beautiful nor read as well.
To Kate Flather and Bottom Feeder, Santa Monica, California for the incredible support.
Also to Alexander and Nora Falk and The Ajam Family for their very generous support.
To Andrew and Jill Miller, Steve and Karen Solomon, Melanie Biggar Andrews,
Fred and Rae Wakelin, Donna and Hunter Craig, The Pingree Family,
Kevin Michael McGuire, and The Nye Family, who made significant contributions that helped fund this book.
And to all 271 backers of my Kickstarter campaign for helping raise the necessary capital to print the book.
A special thank you to my parents, Steve and Miri Oren,
who bought me my very first camera and have supported all of my hopes and dreams.

ISBN 978-0-615-98793-4

Text and photographs copyright © 2014 by Eyal Oren
All rights reserved
This book, or parts thereof, may not be reproduced in any form without permission of the author
Published by Wednesdays in Marblehead, LLC
http://www.wednesdaysinmhd.com

Printed in China

First edition
Book design by Amy Drinker, Aster Designs
The text of this book is set in 10-point Minion Display with Kozuka Gothic headlines

10 9 8 7 6 5 4 3 2 1

CONTENTS

Introduction • 5

Abbot Hall • 6

Beaches • 18

Traditions • 36

From the Rooftops • 46

From the Water • 54

Marblehead Harbor • 64

Marblehead Light • 80

Little Harbor and Islands • 94

Marblehead Neck • 106

Historic Downtown • 116

Parks and Ponds • 126

Introduction

My wife and I moved our family to Marblehead, Massachusetts, in May 2008 so that I could begin work as a physician at the Asthma and Allergy Affiliates in Salem and Danvers. Within months of moving, I began to discover the incredible beauty of our new hometown. In that first year, I also came to realize that, while relatively small, Marblehead had a number of locations that would take time and dedication to explore properly. In August 2010, I started a website with the goal of sharing a favorite image of Marblehead on a weekly basis. As my work schedule offered me a day off on Wednesday, the name of the project quickly became clear…Wednesdays in Marblehead.

It was only six weeks after starting the website that I found the weekly posts inadequate to share the growing number of images I was capturing. That first year found me heading to the top of Abbot Hall with the "cranks," sailing the waters around Marblehead with neighbors, and otherwise exploring the splendor of this New England town. In the second year of the website, I started a number of themed projects to explore the town further through new techniques or vantage points. These included Long Exposure Tuesdays, From the Rooftops Thursdays, and Keep it Local Fridays.

What you will find in these pages are my favorite images of Marblehead captured from 2008 to 2014. One of the most incredible aspects of shooting this town has been realizing what a difference time of day, tide, or season makes in utterly transforming a scene. The byline for my website reads: "An exploration of the beauty of Marblehead, Massachusetts." I hope that, as you turn these pages, you come to share my view of Marblehead as a truly beautiful New England town.

Live Tie-Up Only
The launch at the end of Village Street offers tie-ups for dinghies and larger boats throughout the warm months. It is also a great place to enjoy the sunset as it reflects off the homes along Nonantum Road. *May 24, 2008 7:55 PM*

Abbot Hall

Whether punctuating the skyline or serving as the focal point, Abbot Hall stands out as one of Marblehead's defining landmarks. This is the second Town Hall: the first was constructed in 1727 (now known as the Old Town House), but the town had outgrown it by 1876. In that year, the cornerstone for Abbot Hall was placed, and it opened as the center of town government in 1877. The building is also home to the "Spirit of '76" painting.

The Iconic Beauty of Abbot Hall
The east facade of Abbot Hall offers an imposing view of this beautifully crafted building. This image is a six-minute exposure, which helped to blur the clouds and made for beautiful streaks in the sky. *July 27, 2013 3:07 PM*

Moon over Abbot

The Supermoon was so called because it marked the closest proximity between the moon and Earth in the past 18 years. The close orbit made the moon appear unusually large, and I sought to capture this rare astronomical event as the moon rose. The next morning, I returned to capture the moonset from Chandler Hovey Park and watched as it descended along the perfect path to cross behind Abbot Hall. *March 20, 2011 6:35 AM*

From the Attic of Abbot Hall

This is the incredible view from the east-facing window in the attic of Abbot Hall. You can make out the harbor and lighthouse lying beyond the nearby houses. I felt privileged to have a chance to view, let alone capture, images from this unique spot.
January 19, 2011 11:32 AM

Snow-Capped Houses and Abbot Hall (opposite)

After a blizzard dropped almost two feet of snow, Marblehead was transformed under the beauty of the fresh fallen powder. The houses seen here appear to be stacked on each other and lead the eye toward Abbot Hall towering above. *February 9, 2013 4:23 PM*

First Sail of the Season

In April, before boats fill the moorings of Marblehead Harbor, sailors begin practicing within the protected waters. In this case, the Marblehead High School team can be seen crossing in front of Abbot Hall under soft afternoon light. *April 1, 2012 12:40 PM*

Reflections of Fall Colors (opposite)

2013 was a great year for foliage, and on this day a tree on the grounds of Abbot Hall had reached peak color. By using the large windows of this house on Middle Street, I was able to capture the reflection of the tree and Abbot Hall. *September 28, 2013 11:01 AM*

Abbot Hall under the Tree

As I walked by the tree at Crocker Park after shooting a beautiful sunrise, I discovered that Abbot Hall could be seen under its full canopy. The great morning light cast a nice glow on Abbot Hall tower and the grass in the foreground. *August 3, 2013 5:52 AM*

The Crank Room

Every Thursday morning, the "cranks" meet in the lobby of Abbot Hall before heading up a small elevator followed by two sets of ancient wooden ladders. The destination is the crank room, which houses the machine used to lift huge weights that mark time for the large clock. The room serves as a testament to all of the Marbleheaders who have taken part in this weekly ritual over nearly 150 years.
March 24, 2011 8:22 AM

Abbot's Bell (opposite)

The 1877 bell in Abbot Hall's clock tower is inscribed with the following:
> Presented by James J.H. Gregory to Marblehead, his native town.
> I ring at twelve the joyful rest of noon;
> I ring at nine to slumber sweet of night;
> I call freemen with my loudest tones,
> "Come all ye men and vote the noblest right."

March 24, 2011 8:26 AM

Towering in the Fog

On a spring evening, dense fog appeared in Marblehead Harbor. At this point, the sun had traveled to a perfect position just over Abbot Hall, and the fog lifted just enough to make for a jaw-dropping view. With backlighting from the sun, the wisps of fog were beautifully illuminated, as were the shadows of Abbot Hall and tower. *May 6, 2013 7:14 PM*

Harvest Moon and Abbot Hall

The Harvest Moon rose behind a series of cloud banks in 2011. This was the view from the corner of Village Street and Highland Terrace. The moon was briefly visible between the clouds as it came level with Abbot Hall tower. *October 11, 2011 5:53 PM*

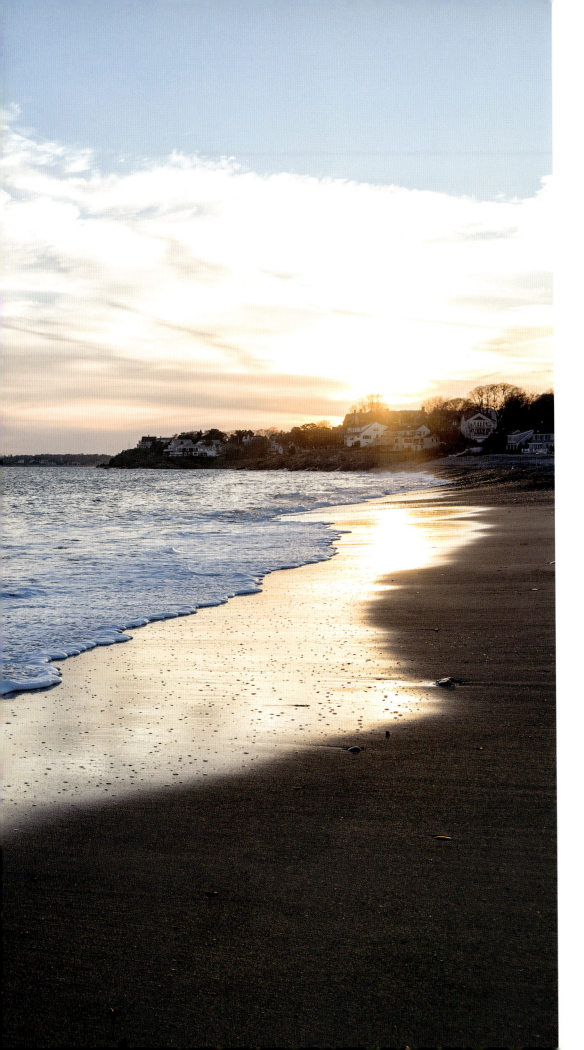

Beaches

Numerous beaches (named, unnamed, private and public) line the shores of Marblehead. Among the most notable are Devereux, Fort, Gashouse, Goldthwait, Grace Oliver, Greystone, Preston, Riverhead, and Stramski's. While the beaches are a popular spot to cool off on those hot summer days, they offer incredibly beautiful views throughout the year.

November Sunset over Devereux Beach
The waves had a great froth to them as they came to shore, and I timed this shot to capture the reflection left in the still-wet sand as a new wave approached. The leading line of ocean surf starting in the bottom left corner leads the eye toward the setting sun as hints of golden light are reflected in the white surf. *November 18, 2012 3:53 PM*

The Lifeguard Chair on Devereux Beach

In the summer of 2011, the three lifeguard chairs on Devereux Beach were painted a brilliant red. Near the end of the night, I saw this composition and captured the chair under a soft pink sky with the causeway beyond and flags hanging from the lampposts.
July 16, 2011 8:27 PM

Summer Swim under the Light of the Moon

By mid-July, the ocean had warmed enough to invite sunbathers into the water. The woman in the distance seems to be pointing up toward the moon as the sunset bathes the clouds in a pink glow. *July 15, 2013 8:27 PM*

Rainbow over the Ocean at Devereux Beach

After a fast storm rolled through town in early summer, a beautiful rainbow could be seen in the distance at Devereux Beach. The rainbow couldn't have been better placed, hovering just over Tinker's Island. The causeway and lampposts can be made out in the distance, there's a bird in just the right spot and, if you look really carefully, you can just make out the double rainbow to the right.
June 8, 2012 5:35 PM

Waves Coming Ashore at Devereux Beach

At this time of year, Devereux Beach is typically deserted at sunset, and the path of the sun is such that it sets behind the houses on the Goldthwait end of the beach. On this particular day, the clouds had moved into place to reflect the light of sunset, and the waves had a nice white frothy crest as they reached the shore. *December 4, 2011 4:03 PM*

Walkway to the Clouds—Goldthwait Reservation (opposite)

This is one of the walkways leading over the rocks and down to the beach at Goldthwait Reservation. On this cloudy day in May, the elements all seemed to come together—from the wood planks to the smooth rocks and the darkening clouds overhead. *May 5, 2011 5:51 PM*

Two Seconds at Grace Oliver Beach

A storm coincided with the full moon on this day, which meant storm surges and high waves. This image was taken near high tide from the road facing Grace Oliver Beach. A 10-stop filter was used to block most of the light and allow for this two-second exposure as a wave crashed and receded. *April 17, 2011 10:29 AM*

Dawn over Preston Beach

The anchor at Beach Bluff Park offers a great focal point for this view of Preston Beach. The dawn light and thick clouds bathed the entire scene in a mix of orange, pink, and red. Ram Island can be seen in the distance. *October 26, 2011 6:58 AM*

Sun Circle at Beach Bluff Park

This image of the sun circle was captured a few minutes after the dawn shot on the opposite page. The colors in the sky had changed drastically in the short time, and the sun had risen into view. The entire structure of the sun circle is visible here with the sun positioned along the edge of one of the slabs to form a sun star. *October 26, 2011 7:10 AM*

Sunrise over Doliber Cove

The sun started to rise on this summer morning in the space between Brown's Island and the edge of Crowninshield Road (with one of my favorite trees visible). The boats in the cove and the swim line added to the scene as the sun's early light reflected beautifully off the clouds overhead. *August 5, 2012 5:52 AM*

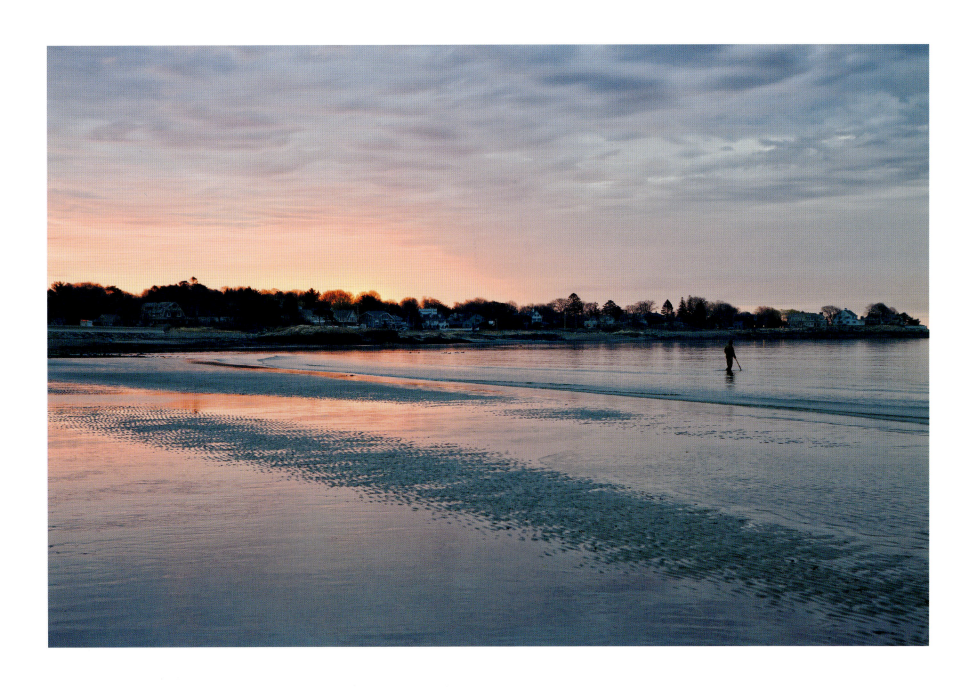

Clamming at Dawn

As the dawn erupted in a cascade of colors, I headed toward Devereux Beach. With the low tide following the new moon, a clammer could be seen making his way through the waters. In this image, a sandbar serves to lead the eye into the scene as the wet sand reflects the morning light. *March 23, 2012 6:45 AM*

Crashing Waves at Greystone Beach

In early March, yet another storm had come to Marblehead and served to stir up the power of the ocean. I composed this image and captured a wave crashing just as the bird flew into the perfect spot in the sky. *March 9, 2013 10:13 AM*

Feel the Waves at Devereux Beach

It was early December and unusually mild on this winter day. I decided to face the camera toward the ocean and photograph the coming waves. This one would end up soaking my feet, and the cold brought me back to reality in a hurry but, for a minute, it sure felt as if summer were just around the corner. *December 4, 2011 4:25 PM*

Capturing the Sunset and Boston Skyline

This panorama including a lone figure shooting the sunset from the small (unnamed) park at the start of Marblehead Neck added a sense of scale and a human touch to the image. With the nice light of sunset and the clear view of the Boston skyline, the final image conveys the feeling of enjoying one of the great views the town of Marblehead has to offer. *November 30, 2013 4:07 PM*

Sunset over the Causeway

On this day, the full moon was due to rise, but clouds had started to fill the sky. I drove to the end of the causeway and pulled over as the sky began to explode in a shower of colors. As soon as the lights of the lampposts turned on, I composed this image to include them and the ledge of the causeway as a leading line into the scene. I pressed the shutter at this perfect moment, when the traffic had died down and the colors reached their peak. *January 15, 2014 4:47 PM*

Dawn Breaks over Castle Rock

In late December, the tide was at just the right height as I set up on the loose rocks at Castle Rock that serve as a beach. In this capture, the waves were caught as they reached the shore, and the moon in the sky clinched it as a favorite. *December 22, 2011 6:41 AM*

Fiery Tendrils Reach out at Devereux Beach

As I arrived at Devereux Beach, I noticed the ocean kept coming in tendril-like motions at certain points. As the sun dipped below the horizon, a red light emanated and was reflected in the temporary pools of water. It almost looks as though the ocean is reaching out with fiery fingers to grab at the shore. *December 23, 2012 4:22 PM*

Traditions

Marblehead is steeped in tradition and continues to highlight many of them formally and informally throughout the year.

Glover's Regiment offers reenactments of times long past during the annual Christmas Walk parade as well as encampments at Fort Sewall over the summer and reimagined battles at other times of the year.

As part of the Fourth of July celebrations, Marblehead begins with the unique lighting of flares that surround the entirety of Marblehead Harbor.

From spring through fall, five yacht clubs fire their cannons at sunset as part of a naval tradition that dates back hundreds of years.

Light up the Harbor
As a prelude to the fireworks celebrating the Fourth of July, Marblehead Harbor is illuminated with flares. Bright red flares, placed by volunteers, line the entire harbor and are set off at dusk. In this image, the dinghies at Fort Beach are seen at low tide with the flares reflected in the still waters and seen extending along the Neck and Chandler Hovey Park in the distance.
July 4, 2011 8:45 PM

Glover's Regiment at the Christmas Walk Parade

During the Annual Christmas Walk, a parade takes place led by Glover's Regiment. As the Regiment turned onto Washington Street, the houses on State Street served as a great backdrop to the scene. The faint traces of falling snow and the wet ground reflecting shadows added to the holiday mood. *December 1, 2012 11:59 AM*

At the Starting Line of the Redd's Pond Model Boat Regatta

The Annual Model Boat Regatta is yet another quintessential Marblehead tradition. The event is put on by the Marblehead Festival of Arts as part of the Fourth of July festivities. Children build and decorate their boats at Abbot Hall before heading to Redd's Pond for the race. *July 4, 2012 3:09 PM*

Fourth of July (opposite)

Chandler Hovey Park offers several vantage points for watching the fireworks explode over the harbor. This was one of the first rockets of the evening. The image was composed so that the colors of the fireworks contrasted with the lighthouse and showcased the distant display across the water. *July 4, 2009 9:12 PM*

Watching the Show from Chandler Hovey Park

This is the first image shared on the Wednesdays in Marblehead website, which launched on August 14, 2010. It remains one of my favorite images of the Marblehead fireworks. The early start added a hint of sunset's colors to highlight the clouds over the first rocket burst. *July 4, 2010 9:08 PM*

Fireworks over the Harbor

Marblehead has been voted in the top 15 locations nationwide to watch fireworks on the Fourth of July. Looking at this scene of people gathered on the rocks of Fort Sewall with the light of the fireworks balanced by the lighthouse and flares illuminating the harbor, it really is no wonder why. *July 4, 2011 9:05 PM*

The Grand Finale

After shooting the beginning of the fireworks display from the rocks at Fort Sewall, I made my way back toward the fort with an idea for the grand finale. I used the great tree as cover to shield the camera's sensor from the brightest parts of the explosions and captured the crowd watching in rapt attention. *July 4, 2011 9:27 PM*

Firing the Cannons at Sunset

Beginning in the spring and continuing until late fall, five of the yacht clubs in Marblehead Harbor follow the naval tradition of colors. The tradition originated with the British Royal Navy and continues with the United States Navy to the present day. The colors refer to the American flag and yacht club burgees, which are raised every morning at 8 AM and lowered at sunset. A gun is fired before the colors are raised and lowered every day except Sunday. The sound of the cannons being fired in succession at sunset has become nearly synonymous with summer in Marblehead.

From May 20 to June 26, I visited each of these yacht clubs and captured their versions of this tradition.

Page 45 top left:
Eastern Yacht Club: *May 20, 2013, 8:02 PM*
Page 45 top right:
Corinthian Yacht Club: *May 30, 2013, 8:11 PM*
Page 44 above:
Boston Yacht Club: *June 3, 2013, 8:15 PM*
Page 45 bottom:
Marblehead Yacht Club: *June 5, 2013, 8:17 PM*
Page 44 right:
Dolphin Yacht Club: *June 26, 2013, 8:22 PM*

From the Rooftops

While riding my bicycle through the streets of historic Downtown in August 2011, I happened to look up and noticed the numerous widow's walks and rooftop decks that graced many of the houses in town. An idea formed to capture a view of Marblehead from the rooftops.

Beginning in September 2011, I was invited into a number of private homes as well as the cupola of Old North Church and once flew in a single prop plane over Marblehead to capture the images I shared on From the Rooftops Thursday. The views never ceased to amaze me, nor did the generosity of all who allowed me into their homes (or church or plane).

Flying over the Neck
On this spring day, I found myself flying over Marblehead in a Cessna 172. The views of familiar landmarks were incredible and this one, of Marblehead Neck, Chandler Hovey Park, Marblehead Rock, and a lone sailboat in the harbor was an easy favorite. *April 25, 2012 4:08 PM*

Sunday Sunrise

On New Year's Day, I joined a new friend at the Old North Church, and the two of us climbed to the cupola for what promised to be a beautiful view of historic Downtown below. We arrived to find the windows of the cupola fogged up but managed to reach fresh air on the bell level just in time. *January 1, 2012 7:26 AM*

Washington Street and Abbot Hall

Shortly before capturing the view to the east from the balcony atop Old North Church, I composed this image facing south. Washington Street is seen from a unique vantage point lined by historic homes and leading the eye toward Abbot Hall in the distance.
January 1, 2012 7:21 AM

Lee Street and the Harbor

This was one of the first private homes I was invited to shoot from. The vantage point was perfect, with views of houses that have stood in these spots for hundreds of years. The harbor is filled with boats, and you can see Marblehead Light in the distance. *September 21, 2011 2:25 PM*

Looking down Washington Street (opposite)

At the end of November, I visited the building on the corner of Washington and Pleasant streets where I spied this amazing view from one of the upper floor windows. There were just enough clouds to diffuse the light of the sun and lend a soft glow to the scene. *November 22, 2011 1:35 PM*

Seeking Grace (opposite)

I looked across from a vantage point on Washington Street and saw this view of Grace Community Church. The houses almost appear to be connected to each other, and the angles of their roofs offer an amazing array of lines leading the eye around the scene.
December 13, 2011 3:54 PM

Peeling Paint and Abbot Hall

This image comes from the same location as "Seeking Grace." As the sun set, the foreground peeling paint and the rooftop architecture became the image's focal point. It is amazing to see the variety of chimneys and follow all of the lines through the photo to the Abbot Hall tower.
December 13, 2011 3:50 PM

From the Water

Though Marblehead offers incredible beauty to be found on land, seeing the town from the water offers a wholly different perspective. Whether it was a trip on a neighbor's sailboat, the Hannah Glover making her way to and from Children's Island, an impromptu excursion on a friend's powerboat, or a bumpy ride on a Zodiac, I have had a number of opportunities to capture views of Marblehead from the water.

Turning the Corner at Brown's Island

In mid-July, a good friend took me out on his boat. As we headed into Doliber Cove, the sky opened up and I saw this perfect scene of Brown's Island with Marblehead Light in the distance. The beautiful golden light, subtle reflection in the water, and the lighthouse in the distance made this an instant favorite. *July 16, 2013 6:56 PM*

Naugus Head from the Water

The view from the water aboard a friend's boat offered me vantage points I had never experienced before and, when we reached Naugus Head, the combination of warm light, calm waters, and the houses peeking out from the canopy of trees added up to a stunning view. *July 16, 2013 6:49 PM*

Fort Sewall from the Water

At the end of July, my family headed out on the Hannah Glover to Children's Island. As we passed Fort Sewall on the left, the combination of great light and clouds made for a picture-perfect chance to capture the fort from a new vantage point.
July 30, 2013 4:23 PM

Out for a Sail

On a Wednesday in the middle of summer, we were invited out for an evening sail by some good friends. This was an early shot taken when we passed a becalmed Sonar drifting toward Chandler Hovey Park and the lighthouse. The positioning of the boat just off to the side and the reflections in the water combined for a classic Marblehead scene. *July 27, 2011 5:49 PM*

Wednesday Night Is for…Racing

The Wednesday Night Series has established itself as a staple of summer in Marblehead. From mid-May to late September, boats of various classes compete in races held just outside the harbor. Shortly after capturing the image of the Sonar on the opposite page, we passed this group of boats making their way out to take part in the evening's races. *July 27, 2011 6:05 PM*

Stand-Up Paddle Through Marblehead

In June 2011, stand-up paddleboarding came to the waters of Marblehead and quickly took hold. I was on Brown's Island when I saw this group float by and took this photo to illustrate just how close you can get to various landmarks by paddleboarding. *August 24, 2011 1:22 PM*

Junior Race Week in Marblehead Harbor

There was little wind to work with as Junior Race Week began in midsummer. The one-person Optis were starting to bunch together and, while that may have been frustrating for the young sailors, it made for fantastic photo opportunities. *July 24, 2013 11:23 AM*

Sunset View from the Water—Marblehead Light and Harbor
As my friend and I made our way back toward Marblehead waters with the goal of entering the harbor, I spotted the sun dipping below the clouds. We slowed at this point, and I waited until Abbot Hall came into view in the distance just over the rocks of Chandler Hovey Park. *July 16, 2013 7:22 PM*

Good Speed and the Corinthian Yacht Club

After capturing the image on the opposite page, we entered Marblehead Harbor and were welcomed with beautiful evening light. As we motored past the Corinthian Yacht Club, I spied this sailboat rocking in the wake of passing boats. Only later did I make out the name of the boat—"Good Speed." *July 16, 2013 7:53 PM*

Marblehead Harbor

Marblehead is home to a beautiful natural harbor with permanent moorings that carry decades-long waiting lists. As the days begin to warm, the harbor slowly fills with boats, reaching peak occupancy in the summer months. The harbor can be appreciated from numerous locations including public ways on Marblehead Neck and a number of parks (Seaside, Hammond, Crocker, Chandler Hovey, and Fort Sewall) and is bordered by Riverhead Beach. The protected waters allow for swimming, kayaking, and stand-up paddleboarding.

A Rainbow over Marblehead Light
In early July, immediately preceding an amazing sunset over the harbor, this cloud and its accompanying rain shower made a brief appearance over Marblehead Neck. I had just enough time to capture this image from Crocker Park as, no more than a few seconds later, the colors began to fade and the rainbow was gone. *July 2, 2012 7:58 PM*

Epic Sunset over Marblehead Harbor

I had made my way to Crocker Park in early July in hopes of shooting the almost-full moon. I watched as this beautiful bank of clouds approached and crossed over the harbor. I captured the breathtaking view of golden light reflecting off the clouds onto the filled harbor below as the moon began to rise over Marblehead Neck. *July 2, 2012 8:14 PM*

Another Epic Sunset over Marblehead Harbor

I had been fortunate to witness and capture some truly astonishing sunsets in the summer of 2012. On this night, I set up on the pier at the Pleon Yacht Club and started shooting toward the setting sun. Then I turned and saw this exceptional light over the lighthouse with clouds that had broken up and reflected nicely over the water. *August 21, 2012 7:41 PM*

The Harvest Moon Rises over Marblehead Harbor

This view comes from atop a roof at the end of Mariners Lane. I could not imagine a more beautiful scene than that of the full harbor with sunset's colors reflected in the still water. And then the Harvest Moon rose over the tree line.
September 19, 2013 6:49 PM

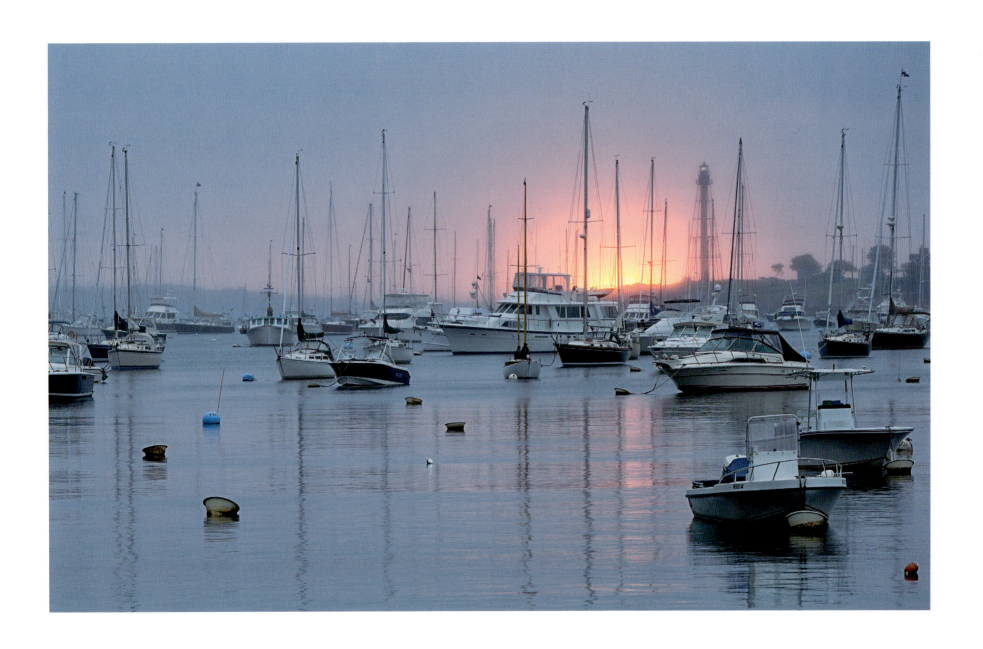

Four-Minute Sunrise over Marblehead Harbor

At exactly 5:03 AM, I saw a hint of pink near the lighthouse from this view at Hammond Park and darted out of the car where I had taken shelter from the rain. The sun reached peak color and brightness at this moment and then, exactly four minutes after it started, the light was snuffed out. *June 12, 2013 5:06 AM*

Lobster Traps and the American Flag

On a late June morning, as I made my way down the ramp to one of the floating docks at the Landing, I noticed the sun was about to rise immediately behind the American flag. I composed this shot balancing the lobster traps in the foreground with the lighthouse and boats in the harbor. The diffused sun behind the flag served to anchor it as a focal point. *June 20, 2012 5:41 AM*

Sunrise on the Summer Solstice
I arrived at Hammond Park at dawn on the summer solstice in time to witness soft pink light fading as the sun began to rise. I composed this image as the sun rose behind clouds and appeared as a red orb. The seagull added a crucial element to the sky at the most opportune moment. *June 20, 2012 5:18 AM*

Best Seat for a Sunset—Chandler Hovey Park

As the sun set on this warm December day, I walked to the edge of the park and composed this image to include the empty harbor and focus on the reflected light off this lone bench. No matter the time of year, Chandler Hovey Park is a great spot to enjoy the magnificent sunsets that bring each day to a close. *December 15, 2012 4:00* PM

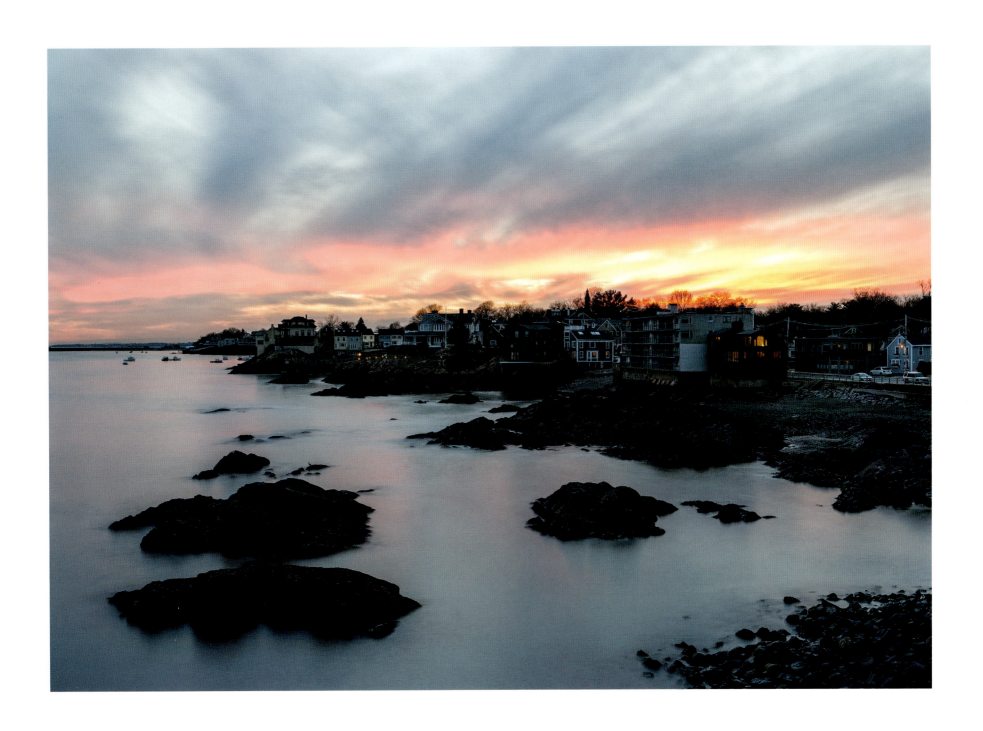

A Late November Sunset over Marblehead Harbor

As the sun set on this November evening, I noticed the light reflecting off the waters of Fort Beach. A fifteen-second exposure served to smooth the water and bring out the reflected colors while adding a bit of motion to the sky. *November 28, 2012 4:19 PM*

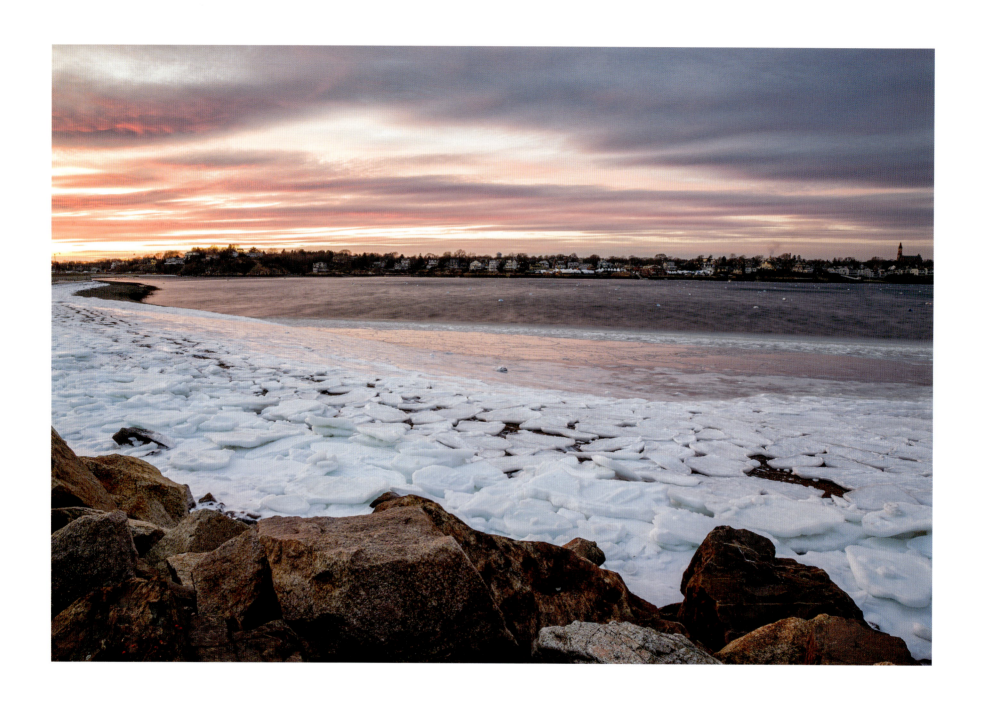

Frozen Marblehead Harbor under Sunset's Light

Throughout this week in January, I noticed that parts of Marblehead Harbor had started to freeze. On this evening, I headed across to the Neck and set up along the rocks facing the harbor at sunset. This was a six-second exposure that served to calm the water a bit and bring out the saturation in the sky. *January 26, 2013 4:56 PM*

Red Sun Rising

I made my way to Crocker Park to capture the sunrise and found dense fog at the horizon. Using a telephoto lens, I composed this view of Marblehead Light and the red sun rising. The fog did wonders for this scene, as did the green light of the lighthouse countering the red light of the sun. *September 11, 2013 6:30 AM*

The Light Show over Marblehead Harbor

June 2012 was a month filled with rainstorms, lightning, and rainbows. This particular evening, I had gone out to Chandler Hovey Park to watch the light show and captured a number of bolts of lightning over the harbor. This is a composite of a few captures of lightning stacked together to highlight Mother Nature's impressive light show. *June 23, 2012 5:17 PM*

Crocker Park on a Warm Summer Day (opposite)

This shot was taken on July 3 when the town was in the midst of a heat wave, and the temperature hit a very muggy 89 degrees. Not surprisingly the float at Crocker Park was packed. Look carefully and you will see five kids caught in midair as they jump into the cool waters of Marblehead Harbor. *July 3, 2013 4:02 PM*

Beaver Moon Rising over Marblehead Harbor

I planned to capture November's full moon (also known as the Beaver Moon) from the Boston Yacht Club. The composition was near-perfect with the brilliant moon, Marblehead Light, and three lobster boats clustered together in rippling water reflecting the soft light of sunset. And then a sailboat magically appeared to complete the scene. *November 16, 2013 4:12 PM*

November Sunset over the Causeway

We enjoyed some incredible sunsets to mark the beginning of November. I had to time this shot so that cars and people wouldn't obstruct the view and ended up with an ideal scene to mark a late fall sunset over the causeway. *November 3, 2013 5:27 PM*

Marblehead Light

Call it what you like but, in the right light, Marblehead Light is a singularly beautiful lighthouse. While it would be difficult to mistake it for a traditional New England lighthouse, the strong lines of its metal frame add a measure of strength to its appearance. The open nature of the structure allows for it to blend seamlessly into the colors of the sky, and yet the central column grounds it firmly to the land of Chandler Hovey Park. A single green light can be seen emanating from atop from dusk till dawn.

Marblehead Light at Sunset
While centering a subject breaks most of the accepted rules of photographic composition, the important part of knowing the rules is understanding when they can and should be broken. In this case there are added elements to distract from the centering of the lighthouse—such as the tree to the left. And the diagonal formed by the pink clouds is accentuated by other diagonals in the reflecting pool of water, ocean, and the lighthouse itself. *June 23, 2012 8:25 PM*

Marblehead Light at Chandler Hovey Park

A friend and I motored out to this point at just the right time, with a subtle backlight bathing Marblehead Light and Abbot Hall in the distance in a soft glow. You can just make out a few boats moored at the mouth of the harbor, but what stands out is the incredible structure of Marblehead Light. *July 16, 2013 7:22 PM*

Sea Smoke

I had never seen (let alone photographed) sea smoke before heading out on a below-freezing morning in January and finding this unbelievable view from Lovis Cove. There was a thick, low-lying bank of clouds, and the sun took a while to come up behind it. When it did, it produced these beautiful touches of light on the smoke and water. *January 15, 2012 7:32 AM*

Doing the Moondance

On this morning, I set out to capture the sun rising over the harbor. As the sun made its ascent, it crossed directly behind the lighthouse at Chandler Hovey Park. The haze helped diffuse the harsh light of the sun, which lit up the sky and waters in a brilliant orange glow. *June 22, 2011 5:12 AM*

Two Stars from the Base of the Lighthouse (opposite)

Standing next to the lighthouse, I was drawn to the red door at its base. As I composed this shot, the sun poked out from behind the clouds and provided me with a perfect sun star to complement the star embossed above the door. *July 5, 2011 7:46 PM*

Marblehead Light Aglow in the Colors of Sunset

When I arrived at Chandler Hovey Park, a great red glow was emanating from the horizon where the sun had just set. I positioned the camera so that the sun's brilliant glow would seem to come from the base of the lighthouse. A few people can be seen at the base, adding a human element and an extra dimension to the image. *May 18, 2013 8:00 PM*

Christmas Comes to Chandler Hovey Park

The park was empty on this cold night as I set up to capture this image over 30 seconds. The longer exposure did wonders for the water and sky, and the relatively still air kept the trees and holiday lights hanging from atop the lighthouse from showing too much movement.
December 23, 2012 4:47 PM

Storm Chasing at Chandler Hovey Park (previous spread)

I went out to chase after big cumulus clouds that had formed over Marblehead Harbor, but they were quickly eclipsed by an approaching cloud formation. The scene was staggering to behold, and I felt as if I were "storm chasing" in the plains. *September 13, 2013 3:18 PM*

Marblehead Light in the Snow

On the last day of December, I headed to Fort Beach after a snowstorm blanketed the town. The holiday lights decorating the lighthouse seemed to blaze in the early evening night, and the still waters of the harbor acted like polished glass to reflect them. *December 31, 2009 4:54 PM*

The Supermoon Rises over Marblehead Light

The Supermoon rose on a Saturday night in March, marking the closest the moon had been to the Earth in 18 years. The proximity made for an even larger full moon, and the atmosphere colored the moon yellow/orange as it rose from the horizon. You can make out a few spectators at Chandler Hovey Park who add a sense of scale to the image. *March 19, 2011 7:16 PM*

Watching the Storm Roll in from Cove Beach

During a break in rain that had fallen all day, I stood at the top of the stairs leading down to Cove Beach. I found this scene under dramatic clouds with a hint of rain in the far left edge of the frame. A few people were enjoying the beach below, and a sailboat was just making its way out to sea. *September 1, 2013 11:48 AM*

Lighting up the Fog at Chandler Hovey Park

On a night with dense fog, I drove to Chandler Hovey Park and was struck by the way the fog accentuated the beams of light as they were split by the branches of this tree. The fog and broken beams of light make for a dynamic scene full of tension, with the light and shadows playing off each other. *December 5, 2013 7:41 PM*

Little Harbor and Islands

Little Harbor spans from Doliber Cove and Grace Oliver Beach past the waters of Gashouse Beach. Brown's Island and Gerry Island offer protection from the Atlantic Ocean beyond, such that the waters can be enjoyed by swimmers, kayakers, and paddlers.

Other islands easily viewed from the shores of Marblehead include Ram, Tinker's, and Children's. There are also a number of named (and unnamed) rocks—among them Marblehead near Chandler Hovey Park and Pig seen off Devereux Beach.

Tinker's Island and the Red Glow of Dawn
The polar vortex was the source of a painfully cold January and, on this day, the arctic air mass was due to envelop Marblehead. As I crossed the causeway, I saw enormous amounts of smoke encircling Tinker's Island and then witnessed a brilliant red glow begin to form. As the first light of the rising sun crested the island, the shallow angle of the sun backlit the sea smoke and made it appear as though the ocean were on fire. The entire sky seemed to catch fire next and turned this fantastic shade of red. *January 4, 2014 7:13 AM*

Sunset over Gerry Island

In mid-June, I found the opportunity to shoot Gerry Island on a night when the sun set near low tide. As if by magic, a small path emerges from the water with each low tide to carry day travelers across Little Harbor. The path formed a gentle S curve to help guide the eye to the small island. *June 20, 2011 7:53 PM*

Morning in Little Harbor

After shooting the sunrise from Hammond Park, I drove toward Little Harbor. I stopped at the boat ramp off Orne Street and watched the boats moored in the still waters. With Gerry Island in the immediate background and the lighthouse jutting out in the distance, the composition came together nicely. *June 12, 2013 7:19 AM*

The Strawberry Moon Rises over Tinker's Island

It wasn't until the moon ascended to this level that it poked through the haze and shone with a red hue that lent credence to two of its given names: Strawberry and Rose Moon. With the aid of a super telephoto lens and the proximity of the full moon to Earth, it appeared to be massive compared to the houses on Tinker's Island below. *June 23, 2013 8:41 PM*

Brown's Island Covered in Snow

I had gone out at high tide after a blizzard swept through town and made my way out to Little Harbor, where I was awed by the level of the water. Before me stood this picturesque view of Brown's Island with pine trees holding onto much of the freshly fallen snow and making for a great contrast. *January 3, 2014 12:27 PM*

Dawn's Light and Tinker's Island
I really couldn't ask for a more beautiful show than the one that lay before me this morning. There were great pink wispy clouds in the sky that reflected in the ocean below. Tinker's Island was surrounded in an orange glow at the horizon, and faint wisps of sea smoke trailed in the distance. *January 25, 2013 6:50 AM*

Purple Dawn from Fountain Park

This was the start of a very foggy early December day in Marblehead. The sky did not disappoint, and the water at high tide served as a great reflector of the purple dawn as seen from Fountain Park. *December 5, 2011 6:41 AM*

Full Rainbow over Ram Island (previous spread)

After a June rainstorm at sunset, a vibrant rainbow developed over the ocean. I headed to Bass Rock Lane, where I saw this marvelous view. The full rainbow was as spectacular as I had ever seen, and I composed this image with Ram Island centered below. *June 17, 2013 7:57 PM*

Clouds Fly over Brown's Island

I headed to Harding Lane for a good vantage point of Brown's Island. This image was taken using a shutter speed of 148 seconds, which allowed the water to blur and the clouds to appear as if they were racing by. The light of sunset reflected nicely off the island and bathed it in a warm red glow. *February 17, 2012 4:53 PM*

Doaks Lane Sunset

I was exploring the area around Gerry Island and Doaks Lane in mid-February. This small corner has become a favorite of mine, with the tree along the shore, the houses that reflect the setting light so well, and the water that often acts as a mirror. In this shot the rocks lead the eye into the scene and the two-minute exposure serves to make the water silky smooth and highly reflective.
February 18, 2012 4:44 PM

Marblehead Neck

Marblehead Neck is connected to the mainland by a two-lane causeway. The Neck is marked by expansive homes as well as three of Marblehead's yacht clubs. Castle Rock can be found on the far eastern shore facing the open expanse of the Atlantic Ocean, while Chandler Hovey Park at the tip is home to Marblehead Light. There is a wildlife sanctuary that is part of the Mass Audubon Society.

A Walk in the Fog
(Best of Show—Marblehead Festival of Arts 2012)
On this night, I found myself on the causeway surrounded by thickening fog that brought out the arc of light from the lamps. As I stood there waiting for cars to pass, a couple made their way toward me. Just as I was about to click the shutter, a car's headlights produced a brilliant glow to backlight and accentuate the figures in the fog. *November 27, 2011 4:44 PM*

Castle Rock Seen from Sky High

Sky High is aptly named as one of the highest points on Marblehead Neck, and here, the castle-like house and Castle Rock itself are seen from this unique viewpoint. *June 3, 2013 7:44 PM*

Dramatic Sky from Castle Rock

In late March, our ocean turned a tropical turquoise hue. I drove to Castle Rock and climbed to a good vantage point from which to photograph the water along this private beach. *March 27, 2013 2:19 PM*

The Tea House on the Neck (opposite)

The founder of the Lipton Tea Company, W. Gardner Barker, built his home on the Neck in the 1880s and settled on this plot of land to do so. As any self-respecting tea maven would, he constructed this exemplary tea house from which to enjoy a morning (or evening) drink. *August 1, 2012 9:36 AM*

The Hydrangeas on Peabody Lane

During a bicycle ride over the Fourth of July weekend, I noticed the beautiful hydrangeas in full bloom at this house on Peabody Lane. As the sun rose above the trees, it produced dappled light to highlight the spectacular blue flowers. This is one of the gardens featured in the Neck's spring garden tours. *July 2, 2011 9:08 AM*

Sunset after the Blizzard

As the Blizzard of 2013 finished dumping 20-plus inches of snow, I drove out to this small park on the Neck. The bench seems to invite the viewer to sit and take in the scene: the ocean waves and mist, the Boston skyline in the distance, and the great colors above.
February 9, 2013 5:15 PM

First Light on an Icy Castle Rock

On this morning, I was surprised to see that the tide pools at Castle Rock had turned to ice. I clambered down to the rocks as the sun began to rise and positioned the camera to achieve this sun star effect. You can make out the reflected warm light in the ice as the sun's rays almost touch the cold mass in the foreground. *January 25, 2013 7:06 AM*

Running to Stand Still

On this particular outing, I drove straight toward the causeway as the clouds seemed to be building over the harbor. As I waited for a break in the traffic, a woman started to run toward me. The sun was throwing long shadows before her and, miraculously, the causeway was momentarily clear of any cars. The wind had picked up just a bit and brought life to the American flags on each of the lampposts.
June 3, 2013 7:21 PM

Exploding Waves at Castle Rock

After Hurricane Sandy passed through town, I decided to head out during the noon high tide to see if the remaining power of the storm might make for some interesting scenes. When I parked at Castle Rock, I was awed by the size of the waves crashing ashore. The lone figure on top of Castle Rock added a crucial element and perspective to the scene. *October 30, 2012 12:38 PM*

Historic Downtown

Called "Old Town" by some, the area of Washington Street as it curves down the hill from Abbot Hall is lined by historic homes (some sharing walls) snuggled in amongst shops, hidden walkways, and historic buildings. The area is also home to the Jeremiah Lee Mansion, Marblehead Arts Association, and Marblehead Museum. Since 1728, the Old Town House has stood at the center of Downtown, built literally in the middle of Washington Street.

In a Fog on Washington Street
(Best of Show—Marblehead Festival of Arts 2013)

In mid-February, a warm-up after a blizzard combined to form dense fog throughout Marblehead. I set out to capture the familiar street, now changed with the darkness of dusk and the diffuse glow of the lampposts in the fog. As I stood in front of the Jeremiah Lee Mansion, a lone gentleman came out from Rockaway Street and walked down Washington Street. As he walked in front of a lamppost, his shadow grew before him and, at the same time, a car came down Washington Street to light up the background fog and houses. *February 11, 2013 8:39 PM*

First Light on the Old Town House

An overnight parking ban extends from the end of fall until early spring. The lack of parked cars removes the element of time from the streets and allows one to imagine the scene as it has been for countless years. I was struck by the solitary location of the Old Town House as the early light touched its top, bathing it in a golden hue. *April 6, 2011 6:37 AM*

Before These Crowded Streets (opposite)

On this morning, I walked the length of Washington Street to the Old North Church and wandered up and down State and Pleasant streets. As the sun rose, the morning light was perfect and turned the Old Town House from its normal yellow exterior to one seemingly painted in gold. *April 6, 2011 6:33 AM*

Early Morning in Historic Downtown

These images of historic Downtown were taken in the early morning hours.

Page 120 top:
The wonderful shops that line this street are lit by the orange glow of street lamps.
December 14, 2010 6:53 AM

Page 120 bottom:
The first house on State Street has seen a great deal of history, as the sign next to its door attests.

   1747: Captain Alexander Watts of Scotland, shipmaster and merchant, built this house and shop on King Street (now State Street).

   1776 to 1803: John Adams, fisherman and mariner, resided and kept a shop. He fought in the American Revolution with Hooper's Seacoast Guards and on the privateer brig Fancy.

   Until 1842: His daughters, Mary and Miriam, ran a successful shop.

   1845 to 1891: The State Street Oyster House, one of Marblehead's finest restaurants, was operated by John Fisher. It then became John Fisher & Son.

   1910: J.O.J. Frost, one of America's finest primitive painters, and his son opened the Frost Home Bakery.

   1959: The King's Rook coffee house was established.

   1988: The building underwent a prize-winning restoration.

April 6, 2011 6:48 AM

Page 121 top:
The Old Town House stands on its own in its brilliant yellow coat. The wreaths on the door add a festive touch. *December 7, 2010 6:48 AM*

Page 121 bottom:
A quiet view of Pleasant Street shows its mix of retail buildings and a church.
December 14, 2010 7:02 AM

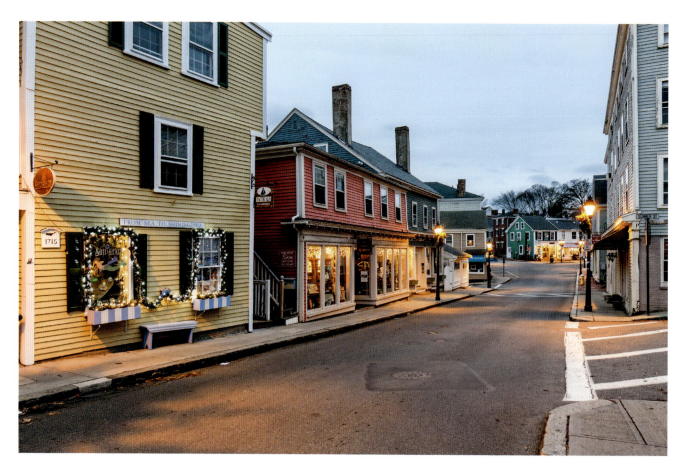

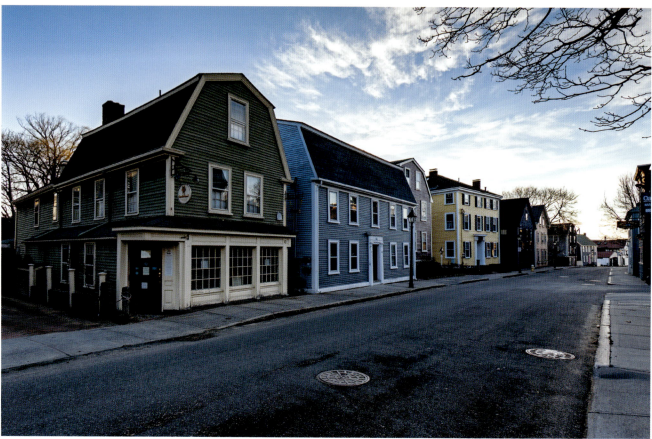

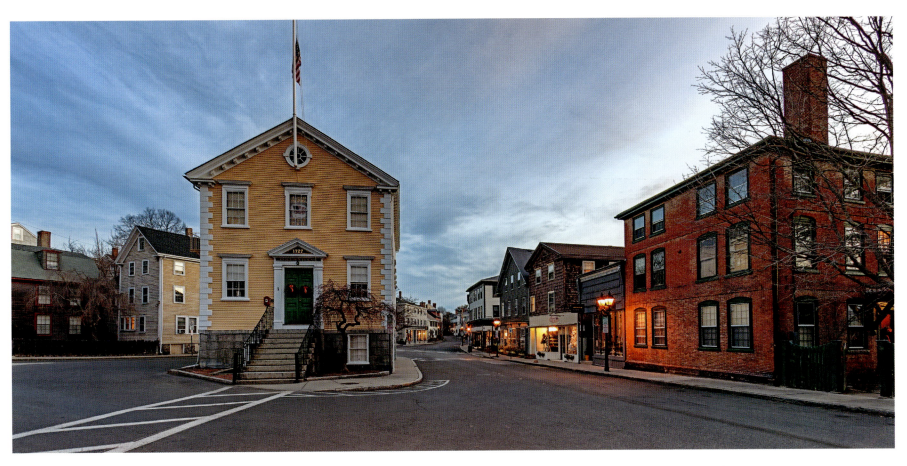

State Street Sunset

The windows of the homes that line State Street reflect the colors of a pink sunset in this view looking up toward Washington Street.
November 10, 2010 4:37 PM

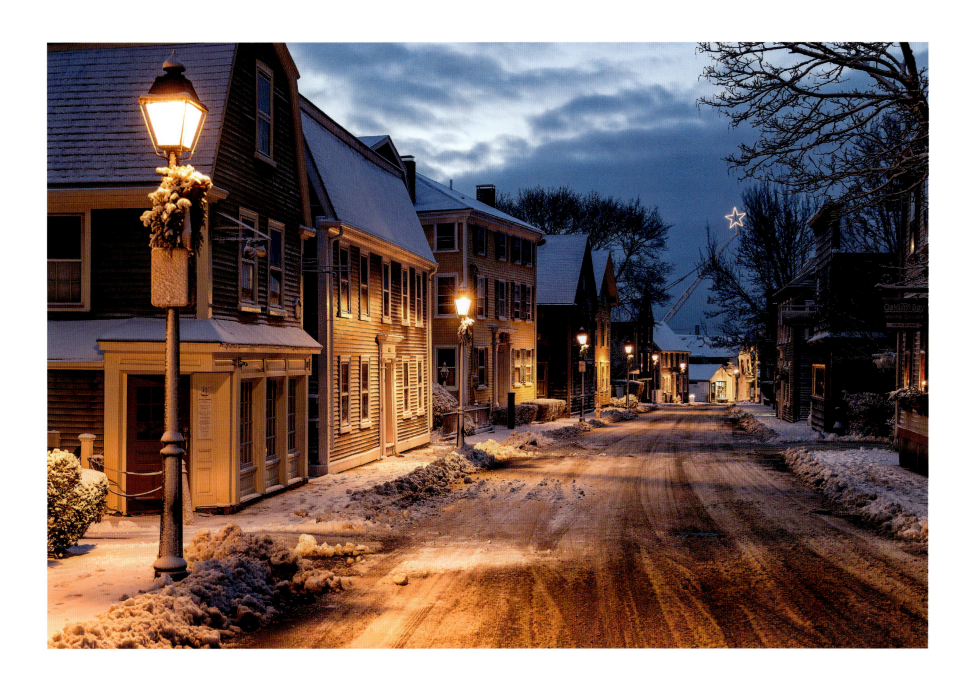

A Shining Star over State Street

The distinguished homes on the curved street, the snow-covered sidewalk, lit street lamps with their wreaths, and that star shining in the sky created the quintessential depiction of "December in Marblehead." *December 30, 2012 6:41 AM*

The Old Town House Blanketed in Snow (opposite)

Just the right amount and type of snow brought out the beauty of the Old Town House on this day. The road was clean, the streets were empty, and even the Do Not Enter sign was covered just enough not to serve as a distraction. *December 30, 2012 7:45 AM*

Snow on Washington Street

I stopped here for the composition of Abbot Hall tower rising over the storefronts on Washington Street. The classic scene was made more beautiful with the blanket of white. *December 30, 2012 7:52 AM*

Parks and Ponds

A number of parks and ponds dot the landscape of Marblehead, including Crocker Park overlooking the harbor; Chandler Hovey Park, where Marblehead Light is located; Fountain Park, offering expansive views of Little Harbor; Hammond Park, abutting the harbor; Memorial Park; and Seaside Park. Fort Sewall and Castle Rock offer additional magnificent views of the town and surrounding waters. Not to be forgotten, Marblehead's ponds have their own unique appeal and include the classic Redd's Pond as well as Black Joe's, Ware, Hawthorn, and several unnamed ones.

Fort Sewall in the Snow
A significant storm passed through Marblehead, and I made my way up to Fort Sewall to explore. The snow was wet and the air still so the tree that stands in front of the red doors still held on to much of it. The beautiful outline of the tree's bark and the red doors offering a touch of color made for a flawless scene. *January 18, 2009 3:30 PM*

Falling Snow on Redd's Pond (previous spread)

On Wednesday, January 16, a snowstorm was predicted for Marblehead. I arrived at Redd's Pond while the snow fell and captured the flakes as they blanketed the pond. *January 16, 2013 7:36 AM*

Melting Ice at Redd's Pond

This image was taken during a spring thaw as Redd's Pond began to melt. The familiar red house reflecting in the waters and the subtle clouds in the blue sky combined for an incomparable late winter/early spring scene. *March 3, 2009 3:32 PM*

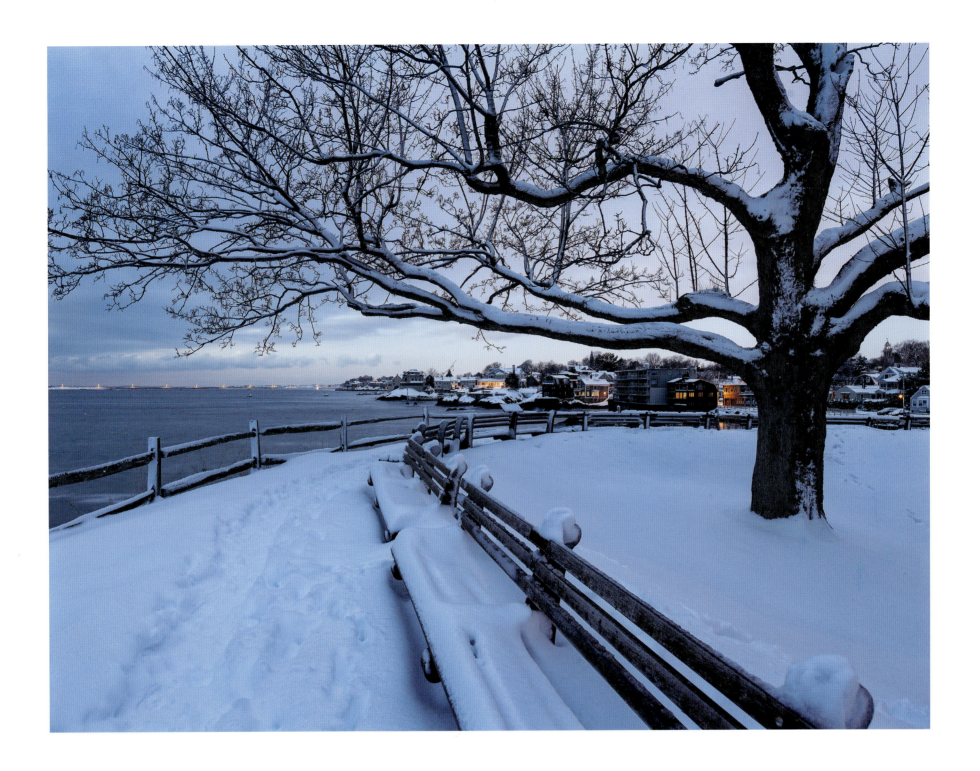

Snow at the Fort

I arrived at Fort Sewall the morning after a snowstorm to find this beautiful scene before me. The great tree had held on to much of the fallen snow, and the blue light at this time of morning did wonders for the view. In the distance, the causeway's lampposts shone their orange lights, which balanced well against the lights of the homes along Front Street. *February 6, 2014 6:23 AM*

An Incredible Dawn from Crocker Park

On this morning, I headed to Crocker Park as the sky started to build with color. I ran to the top of the hill just as the colors of dawn had reached their peak. I chose this composition, including the rocks of Crocker Park, the boats in the harbor, and Marblehead Light in the distance all lit by the pinks, oranges, purples, and blues coloring the sky above and waters below. *August 3, 2013 5:27 AM*

Morning Comes to Crocker Park

After capturing the image on the opposite page, I sought a composition including the trees that stand near the flagpole, while keeping the harbor and lighthouse in strong positions in the frame. This spot was ideal, and I couldn't have asked for better light.
August 3, 2013 5:30 AM

Sunset from Fort Sewall Overlooking Marblehead Harbor

As I walked back along the path toward the tree at Fort Sewall, I noticed these great undulating clouds forming over Marblehead Harbor. I sought to capture the beautiful structure of the clouds and was thrilled with the way the pink light of sunset reflected off them. *June 6, 2013 8:25 PM*

Fall Regatta at Redd's Pond

As I drove up Pond Street on this fall morning, I happened upon a regatta taking place at Redd's Pond. I set up for a view to include the backdrop of the house across the pond and Old Burial Hill. As the boats came by under ideal conditions, I captured this pair in the foreground. *October 7, 2012 10:45 AM*

Gravestones and Cherry Blossoms at Harris Street Cemetery

The cherry trees at Harris Street cemetery reached peak bloom in late April, and I found myself drawn back to them morning and night for three consecutive days. Here you can see the blossoms at full color framed by the ancient grave markers and the steeple of Grace Community Church. *April 24, 2013 7:02 PM*

Spring Comes to Washington Street (opposite)

Cherry blossoms are forever intertwined with feelings of springtime for me, and this tree in particular marks the first day of spring in my mind whenever it chooses to bloom. *April 24, 2013 5:29 PM*

The Harvest Moon Rises over Marblehead Harbor

When I arrived at Crocker Park to capture the year's Harvest Moon, I was thrilled to see that the honey locust tree had started to show off its fall colors. I decided to compose my shot to include the tree and help place the time of year. *September 30, 2012 6:37 PM*

Running in the Fog at Fort Sewall

As the sun rose on this foggy day, the sky took on a magical orange hue. After I had composed this image with a few boats visible through the fog, someone out for a morning run came into the frame. The addition of the human element added greatly to the composition and ended up being one of my favorites from this morning. *September 11, 2013 7:06 AM*

Foliage in the Fog at Seaside Park

This maple tree at Seaside Park was in the wrong light when I had visited it a few days earlier. The light was perfect on my return and the fog brought an extra dimension to the scene. The tree was displaying magnificent color, and I lined up the memorial stone and sign with the scoreboard in the distance huddled between the two. *October 20, 2012 8:21 AM*

The Pond off Whittier Road

I could not have asked for more picture-perfect conditions on a great fall day in Marblehead. Every element came into place, and I found this composition accentuated each piece. *October 23, 2013 10:54 AM*

A Canopy of Snow on Glendale Road (opposite)

The classic New England scene of a canopy of trees contrasted with freshly fallen snow is made more special by the hint of dawn's colors in the sky above. *February 6, 2014 7:05 AM*

After the Storm—Lovis Cove at High Tide

As I drove down Front Street, the way to Fort Beach was closed due to flooding. At Lovis Cove, the snow pushed against the wall and frozen sea water caked on the bordering buildings highlighted the frigid temperature. The metal chain along the wall pulls the eye toward the water at peak high tide. *January 3, 2014 1:00 PM*

The Barnacle

A 150-second exposure turned the crashing waves at Lovis Cove into a white smoky mist. The colors of sunset were made deeper and more vibrant, and the clouds that had been in the sky were transformed into long streaks of light. *November 10, 2010 4:16 PM*